Old DALMELLINGTON, PATNA & W₁

by
Donald L. Reid

Dalmellington, *c.*1904. This view was taken from the Cocky Knowe which is where the roadway to Bellsbank housing estate was cut in 1948 from the main Dalmellington–Carsphairn road in the foreground. The building immediately on the left of McClymont's Bridge was known locally as 'Rory's Den', and housed many local families. It was demolished in the late 1950s and a nursing home now stands on the site. The cattle on the right are in a field formerly owned by Mr Colville, a local grain merchant and farm supplier. In the days before motorised transport, cattle and sheep being driven between Ayr and Galloway would often rest and graze in Dalmellington before continuing their journey. The parish church, in the background, was built in 1846 from Dunaskin sandstone and was dressed and built by local masons. The Muck Burn runs through the centre of the village and over the years heavy rains resulted in extensive flooding on several occasions.

This Chevrolet bus, which was new in 1929, was owned by William Newall of the Mill, Dalmellington; his son Tom (pictured) was the driver. The bus worked local routes such as the steep climb from Dalmellington via Burnton and Craigmark to the village of Benwhat, located on the high moorland plateau above Dalmellington. Benwhat was built by the Dalmellington Iron Company to house miners and workers at the Dalmellington Ironworks at Waterside, but the population began to transfer to houses in Dalmellington between 1948 and 1955.

ISBN 1 84033 149 6

The publishers regret that they cannot supply copies of any pictures featured in this book.

The author's fee for writing this book has been donated to
The Dalmellington Band

This book is respectfully dedicated to the author's uncle
Donald Lees Reid
1930–2001
of North Beoch, Dalmellington, and Barnsley, who never forgot his mining roots. He loved the Doon Valley, especially Dalmellington. "May the sons of our sons remember Dalmellington with pride"

ACKNOWLEDGEMENTS

The author is indebted to the following individuals for their kind assistance in the compilation of this book: Kate Adamson, Edward Barclay, Jim Bowie, John Collins, John Dinwoodie, Hugh Hainey, Giles Hutchison, John Hutchison, Annie B. Joss MBE, John H. 'Ian' Killin, Patrick McCutcheon, William McHendry, Robert McSporran, David Rarity, James and Mary Reid, Iain Shaw of Houston, Stanley Sarsfield and Tom Smith. Special mention must be made of Hugh Johnstone MBE for his help. Hugh is a remarkable man whose pride and joy is the Dalmellington Band.

The publishers and author wish to thank the following for contributing photographs to this book: Robert Grieves for the front cover and page 2; Alex McGowan for pages 1, 4, 6, 10, 11, 13, 19, 20 (right), 23, 24, 30, 31, 33 (left), 38, 41, the inside back cover and the back cover; Jean Kennedy for pages 9, 25–27, 35 and 43; Hugh Johnstone for page 18; Giles Hutchison for page 44 (both); John Dinwoodie for page 48; and Terry Harrison for page 34.

INTRODUCTION

The upper section of the Doon Valley has a fascinating industrial and social history. Dalmellington can be traced as far back as 1003 when there was some settlement at its present location and mention is made of a church there in the records of the Diocese of Glasgow towards the end of the thirteenth century. It is known that this church was situated in the old graveyard below the motte at the east end of the village, but no trace of it exists today. The origins of the village name can be read in two ways, either as *Dal Muilean Tuin*, 'the fort on the plain of the mills', or *Dal Meallan Tuin*, 'the fort on the plain of the hills'. There is evidence for either translation as there are both mills and hills, while 'fort' refers to the motte, known locally as the Mote, which was probably built by ancient Pictish inhabitants.

The village was located on an ancient route which linked the Old Edinburgh Road with the pilgrim way to Whithorn, a location which in the seventeenth century left it caught between a strong royalist presence at Carsphairn and a very active Covenanting one in Cumnock. In 1685 six hundred troops were quartered in the parish, causing considerable upset to the local population of a few hundred with whom they were billeted. Fines were levied on those caught at Conventicles and people were also imprisoned, families dispersed, and houses plundered because local men had stood up against Episcopacy. Many of these men, especially those from the farming community, became involved with the Covenanters. Quintin Dick, an elder in the parish church, was one who suffered terribly during those years. He was imprisoned in 1684 and a year later was taken from Edinburgh to be detained in Dunottar Castle. He would have been deported, but was left behind because it was believed he was dying. He recovered and returned to Dalmellington where he endeavoured to heal the differences which had separated the Presbyterian brethren of the parish.

For many, Dalmellington is synonymous with Loch Doon which is located 3 miles south of the village. Loch Doon Castle is of ancient origin and the Galloway Picts used Castle Island to fight off an invasion by the Cambrian Celts in the fourth century. In 1823 nine ancient Pictish canoes, made of hollowed oak, were discovered. Three of the canoes were recovered and one was sent to the Hunterian Museum in Glasgow. In 1306 and 1319 the castle was besieged by the English, who periodically invaded southern Scotland for some time after the Battle of Bannockburn, but it was said that the castle remained impregnable. However, during the reign of James V, who endeavoured to curb the powers of local barons, the castle was finally burned down and never rebuilt. During the construction of Loch Doon Dam between 1934 and 1936 the water level of the loch was substantially raised and the ruin was removed stone by stone from the island and rebuilt on the west side of the loch where it stands today. The foundations at the former site on the island can also still be seen when the water level of the loch is low.

In 1916 an attempt was made to construct a School of Aerial Gunnery at the loch. Despite the warnings of the area's notoriously poor weather, the planners went ahead and hangers, roads and jetties were built and the level of the loch was raised. However, in the end the weather won and the project had to be abandoned. A subsequent parliamentary inquiry concluded that 'Loch Doon will be remembered as the scene of one of the most striking instances of wasted expenditure [in excess of £3 million] that records can show'. An airfield covering some 88 acres was also constructed at Bogton on the western edge of the village and this remained an operational airfield until the end of the First World War. The remains of the hangers can still be seen on this site.

By the eighteenth century handloom weaving had become one of the staple cottage industries, but in the following century this trade went into decline and was replaced by the growing mining industry. From 1848 the Dalmellington Iron Company and its successors operated dozens of pits and drift mines in the valley to extract coal and ironstone, and many people will remember the names of Bowhill, Polnessan, Dalharco, Houldsworth, Jellieston, Burnfoot, Drumgrange, Dunaskin, Corbie Craigs, Craigmark, Minnivey, Bogton, Sillyhole, Chalmerston, Pennyvenie, Clawfin, Benbain and Beoch, all of which had underground workings. In all there have been 43 local pits from the 1840s until the present day when all that remains is extensive opencast mining overlooking the east of the village.

Three miles north of Dalmellington is Waterside which was once a thriving industrial village. Massive chimneys, at 143 and 160 feet respectively, still dominate it, and these, along with the ironstone bing, are reminders of the extensive mining and iron producing activities of the Dalmellington Iron Company there. High above Dunaskin Burn is the site of Laight Castle. According to tradition it was here that the army of Alpin, King of Scots, met the Alcluydian Britons of Strathclyde in a fierce and bloody battle which ended with the death of the Scots king. Today only two rows of houses remain at Waterside, but its industrial heritage is on display at the nearby open air museum which aims to preserve the industrial and social history of the village.

Two miles north of Waterside is Patna. Some historians have claimed that the name is derived from *Pait 'n Ath*, 'the water of the eminence', for the old village was built upon a steep hillside west of the River Doon, but it is more likely that the village received its name from its founder, William Fullarton, whose family had connections with the city of Patna which stands on the River Ganges. Like its near neighbours, Patna relied heavily on coal mining and remained a very small village until the inhabitants of Lethanhill and Waterside were rehoused there in the mid-1950s.

Today these villages lack any significant local employment and most people travel to Ayr or further afield to find work. However, the Scottish Industrial Railway Centre at Minnivey, where some excellent locomotives have been preserved, has helped to attract tourists. Similarly, there are major works ongoing at Waterside to further develop and enhance the 'Dunaskin Experience', Europe's best example of a nineteenth century ironworks. Both museums work together and it is hoped that steam engines will shortly work between Waterside and Dalmellington. Tourism is also being encouraged by Dalmellington's current Book Town initiative and the town now has various antiquarian bookshops located within part of the old High School site. However, a large employer of local labour is undoubtedly of the greatest need to help regenerate an area of historical significance and outstanding natural beauty.

Dalmellington Bowling Green, pictured in the foreground, was established in 1875 while the open ground to its right later became the King George V football park, used by local amateur teams. In the centre background on the plateau above Dalmellington can be seen Benbraniachan with Chalmerston pit just to the left in front. Extensive opencast mining has resulted in the complete removal of Benbraniachan. By 1930 some 250 miners were winning coal at Chalmerston Nos. 4, 5 and 6. Nos. 4 and 5 were opened in 1924 and continued until 1959 while No. 6 opened in 1925 and closed in 1935. On the upper left of the photograph can be seen Burnton village which was constructed by the Dalmellington Iron Company between 1924 and 1926 and consisted of 88 houses. For fourteen years following Burnton's completion the people of Craigmark were transferred there so that their old village could be demolished. The local cinema, built in 1935, is the large building between the church and Burnton. It became a bingo hall in the 1960s and was demolished in the 1970s. A sheltered housing complex now stands on the site.

This photograph was taken from Knoweview around 1910. Broomknowe houses, constructed that year, can be seen in the clearing left of centre but there are no sign of houses at Burnton. Behind the tennis court, which was built after the First World War and survived until 1933, is the row of weavers' cottages which now house the Cathcartston Museum. This regularly displays local heritage exhibitions, endeavouring to preserve the social history of the district.

High Church Street is one of the steepest braes in the village and now leads to Dalton Avenue which was built at the top of this road in the 1950s. The house on the right is Duneian Cottage which was occupied by Robert Thomson, bandmaster of Dalmellington Band from 1911 to 1927. Originally from Fife, Mr Thomson was conductor of Burnieknowe Band, based between Lugar and Auchinleck, and took up his appointment with Dalmellington after Albert Carr retired in 1910, having successfully led the band for almost 30 years. The band was formed in 1864 and the bandmaster was always supplied with a rent-free house and a job in the local pits.

Knowehead, or the 'Windy Row' as it is affectionately known by Dalmellingtonians. Designed to seat 900, the parish church was erected in 1846 at the expense of Mrs McAdam Cathcart of Craigengillan. The former church, built in 1766, became the church hall. One of the church's ministers was Rev. George S. Hendrie who served the parish from 1880 to 1925. He was keen to promote the village to tourists and believed that it had the potential to become a spa town. In 1889 he even published a guide to the district in which he stated his hope that 'the day will come when Dalmellington people will see it to be more for their interest to provide the necessary accommodation for these and other summer visitors'. At the time of the union of the Church of Scotland and the Free Church of Scotland in 1926, the parish church became known as the Kirk o' the Covenant and the former free church became Lamloch Church. The Kirk o' the Covenant has a very valuable collection of Covenanter silver, including small cups dating from 1637 and 1650 which are reputed to have been taken by Rev. Alexander Stevenstone (1648–1680) into the nearby hills at Benbeoch Craig where they were used to give communion at Conventicles.

High Main Street viewed from the Square. The cottage on the immediate left will be remembered by elder villagers as being Dr Lees's surgery for many years. High Main Street was dominated by shops belonging to Dalmellington Co-operative Society which was established in 1879. By 1951 the society employed 71 people and had a membership of 1,455 with an annual turnover of £144,000. The high buildings on the right were occupied by the grocers, drapers, bakers and butchers, while the highest building on the right was the Co-op bakery. The Co-op boot and shoe shop was the second building on the left; in the 1940s Fyfe the chemist took over the premises, and by the 1960s it had become Hay's the chemist. The building is now derelict.

MAIN ST, DALMELLINGTON.

Main Street, c.1910, with the Eglinton Hotel on the right. This was an old coaching house and stabling was provided at the rear of the hotel. On the opposite side of the road from the hotel was Dalmellington Railway Station. In 1848 the Ayrshire & Galloway Railway Company began construction of a line from Ayr to Dalmellington, but they were besieged with financial and legal problems. The Glasgow & South Western Railway Company became involved, bringing the project to fruition, and on 15 May 1856 the Dalmellington Iron Company were able to deliver their first load of pig iron to Ayr on the new line. Passenger services began on 7 August 1856, a great day of celebration in Dalmellington. Just seven weeks later, however, there was a major collision near Cutler Bridge at Waterside. The points had been incorrectly set and a passenger train crashed into a rake of Iron Company wagons, causing injury to five passengers and the guard. The man who had failed to set the points was imprisoned for four months and the driver of the train received two months because he had exceeded the speed limit of 4 m.p.h. Passenger services to Dalmellington ceased on 6 April 1964 and the station closed completely on 6 July the same year.

Shortly after the Boer War a Mrs McGarva owned the prominent house on the left called Castle Dudley. The famous brass band composer, J.A. Greenwood, composer of the trombone solo 'The Acrobat,' was resident in Castle Dudley at the time he tutored the Dalmellington Band for their participation in the Ayrshire Brass Band Association contest at Maybole in 1904. The building close to Castle Dudley and facing onto the Carsphairn Road was used as a school house from the mid-1850s until the building of Dalmellington High School in 1875. The High School was erected at the expense of Mr McAdam of Craigengillan and he also paid the salary of the headmaster for the first ten years. The High School was replaced by a modern building in August 1875 and renamed Doon High School, later becoming Doon Academy. Many older Dalmellingtonians will fondly recall William B. Irving who was headmaster from 1958 until his retirement in 1971. The last headmaster of the old school was Gordon C. Douglas who took over the position from Mr Irving, retiring when the old school closed.

The Flood, Dalmellington, 11th July, 1927

Rising in Loch Muck, 6 miles south of the village on the road to Carsphairn, the Muck Burn has flooded Dalmellington on several occasions. The flood of 17 July 1927 was particularly bad and this shows crowds gathered near the Square at the foot of High Main Street where the extent of the damage is all too evident with water gushing from the buildings. The long buildings in the picture were replaced by new buildings belonging to the Dalmellington Co-op Society and the Merrick Café and Hall around 1935. The standpipe on the right provided water for the villagers and was part of the gravitational water system opened in 1882 by Mrs McAdam of Craigengillan. Prior to this water was obtained from the burn where women often did their washing.

The Moat, Dalmellington

Valentines Series

The Mote is a circular mound which towers above the village and is in an excellent state of preservation. It has been classified as an ancient monument. On the right of this picture of High Street is Ye Old Castle House, a public house run by a Mrs Gerard prior to 1897 and then by Albert A. Carr, conductor of the Dalmellington Band, who remained the licensee until his death in 1920. The building was then used by various businesses over the years, but is currently unoccupied.

This photograph was probably taken shortly after 1915 when the iron bridge in the background was built in Dalmellington Square. This was built by contractors employed on the construction of the School of Aerial Gunnery at Loch Doon which opened the following year. The iron bridge was removed in 1935 when the Square was reconstructed so that the burn became totally covered over where it passed through the centre of the village. A bridge identical to this one still stands on the Dalmellington–Straiton Road.

The Two Brigs - Dalmellington.

28.

As well as the iron bridge there was also the much older stone one in the centre of the village, but during the construction of Loch Doon Dam between 1935 and 1936, it was found that they could not cope with the heavy industrial traffic caused by this project (the main road which now bypasses the village centre had not then been built). It was therefore decided to create what is now the current Village Square which involved covering over the entire length of the Muck Burn to give more room for traffic.

THE SQUARE AND MAIN STREET, DALMELLINGTON.

Dalmellington Square looking towards Main Street, pictured in the 1950s long after reconstruction. The lorry belonged to John Robertson of Patna who had a thriving milk delivery service in the Doon Valley. The car is a Triumph Mayflower and belonged to Mr McCallum, baker, whose business operated from the premises with the canopy. The shop behind the telephone kiosk was run as a butcher's by Malcolm Ross, who was in business there from the 1920s until around 1965. It is still a butcher's, operated by William Paterson, son of the late owner, James Paterson. The wooden gate marks the location of a small garage which is still owned and operated by James Gibson, but no longer sells petrol. The building on the immediate left of the picture is the Doon Tavern which is still open.

THE SQUARE, DALMELLINGTON.

A.59

Dalmellington Square, looking towards High Main Street. The building in the centre is the Merrick Hall with the Merrick Café on its immediate left. During the 1940s and '50s the hall was a popular venue for dances and social evenings before the community centre was built; today the hall is used as a store for the café. The long building immediately to the right and behind the Merrick Hall was for many years the Orange Hall and sits behind a narrow lane, known as the Path, which runs between Churchhill and the foot of the Mote. The building is now boarded up and not in use. Prior to the demise of the local pits, everyday at 1 p.m. the Square would be busy with miners waiting for buses to transport them to work for the back shift. The gable of the building on the immediate right beside the car is that of the Railway Inn which is still open today.

Castle Crofts, Dalmellington

Castle Crofts probably takes its name due to its proximity to a building, no longer standing, known locally as Dame Helen's Castle which was situated nearby on the banks of the Muck Burn. The crofts were probably the small houses which were occupied by local workers. The house in the centre background is called Invergarry and was occupied in the 1920s and '30s by Alex Glass, clerk to the district council. On the hill in the background runs the Pickan's Dyke, probably some sort of ancient rough fortification and on the left is Ben Beoch.

Dalmellington Band at Carnegie Hall, Dunfermline, 1969. They had just won the Scottish Brass Band Championships with the test piece 'Carnival Romaine', under their conductor and lifelong member, Hugh Johnstone. Hugh Johnstone was a member of the band from his boyhood days and is still an instructor today. In 1982 he was awarded the MBE for his services to the brass band movement and Dalmellington Band continues to be one of the finest brass bands in Scotland. *Back row* (left to right): Donald Tyson, John Tyson, Hugh Uriarte, Tom Paulin, Alex Yates, William Cuthbert, Robert Dunn and Archie Hutchison; *middle row*: Edward Kerr, Robert Boyd, Bert Ritchie, Freddy Galloway, David Sturgeon, Louis Uriarte, Tom Paulin (uncle of other Tom Paulin), Ian Boyle and Willie Hainey; *front row*: William Kennedy, Jim McPhail, Robert Dunn, John McCulloch, Hugh Johstone (conductor), Peter Murray, Jim Graham, Tom Wilson and John 'Jubie' McCulloch.

CRAIGENGILLAN HOUSE DALMELLINGTON

Craigengillan House stands on the west bank of the River Doon in extensive policies which were founded by the McAdam family on the lands known as Berbeth in 1611. The family originally came from the area between Carsphairn and Dalry and Craigengillan had been the name of their former homestead. The McAdams of Craigengillan were a branch of the same family which produced John Loudon McAdam, the great road builder. As he did with so many other members of the landed gentry, Robert Burns addressed one of his epistles to the young laird of his time. The present house was built in 1780 and around 1820 a manorial entrance front was added, together with tall chimneys and the square tower. Adjacent to the house are impressive stables which have a huge domed tower above the entrance arch. The house can be viewed from the Loch Doon road and is a very impressive sight.

The cottage known as the Wren's Nest was located on the Dalmellington–Cumnock road, just past the extensive Pennyvenie coal bing on the edge of Camlarg Estate. It was owned by the Dalmellington Iron Company and was used to house workers from the local pits. Adam Johnstone of Dalmellington occupied the cottage in the 1940s and the last occupant was Alex White. The cottage was demolished in the 1950s.

Camlarg Cottages, which were still thatched in the early 1930s, were known locally as the Collier's Row and were located a short distance from the Wren's Nest near to Pennyvenie Colliery. The row consisted of four separate cottages and were owned by Baird & Dalmellington. They were demolished in the early 1950s. Pennyvenie Farm can be seen in the background This, too, was recently demolished because of the extensive opencast mining operations currently ongoing in the area. A railway line with coal wagons which served Pennyvenie Colliery can be seen between the cottages and the farm.

"A Wayside Thatch", Dalmellington.

BELLSBANK HOUSING ESTATE, DALMELLINGTON.

A.60

Bellsbank housing estate lies a half mile south of Dalmellington, located between Pennyarthur Rig and Bogton. Building of the scheme began in 1948 to provide additional housing for the area to accommodate incoming mine workers. The current population is around 2,000 and there is a primary school, health centre and shops all within the estate. In the early days local people had summer picnics at nearby Parkelly Burn on the western edge of Craigengillan Estate.

The first dam and sluice gates at Loch Doon, 3 miles south of Dalmellington, were built by John McAdam of Craigengillan in 1787 to control the flow of water from the loch and to prevent flooding on the low-lying plain between Dalmellington and Patna. In 1826 McAdam's grandson, Quinton McAdam, was responsible for building the path from the dam, which clings to the side of the mile long Ness Glen above the thundering River Doon, to the quieter and calmer waters at the woodland policies of Craigengillan. The path became a well-known visitor attraction and William Hewitson, the last precenter of Dalmellington Parish Church, was employed as a guide there until his death in 1887. This bridge was later replaced by the Loch Doon Dam in 1935 when major works began in connection with the Galloway hydro-electric scheme. Today the glen is overgrown, blocked by fallen trees, and the erosion of the path has now unfortunately made it unsafe for walkers.

Showing the other side of the bridge, this was the scene at the foot of Loch Doon where it enters the Ness Glen prior to the construction of Loch Doon Dam in the 1930s. During the First World War there was a prisoner of war camp at Loch Doon, the first prisoners arriving in March 1917. At the same time well over 3,000 men employed by McAlpine builders were engaged in building the School of Aerial Gunnery. The German prisoners were used to help construct some of the access roadways, but not the school itself as it was contrary to the Hague Convention to use prisoners of war on specific military works.

Loch Doon Castle is an eleven sided curtain-walled castle designed to defend its original island site at the southern end of Loch Doon. The stonework is outstanding and its beautifully hewed blocks of ashlar have stood the test of time. The original castle dates from the thirteenth or fourteenth centuries, but it is believed that a much earlier settlement was sited on the island. In 1826 nine ancient canoes containing an oak war-club and battle-axe were discovered nearby and some of these relics can be found at the Hunterian Museum in Glasgow. Legend tells that the castle gave shelter to Robert the Bruce who fought battles in the area, most significantly the Battle of Glentrool in 1307. The castle was removed from its island position to the west bank of the loch during 1935 and 1936 when the Galloway hydro-electric scheme threatened to submerge the island. The photograph dates from the early 1900s and shows divers in the water trying to locate the portcullis gates of the castle which were believed to have been thrown into the loch during one of the attacks on the castle in earlier times.

The Dalmellington Iron Company was founded in 1847 by Henry Houldsworth, a Nottinghamshire entrepreneur who made his fortune in the cotton industries in Manchester and Glasgow. After a successful period in the ironworks at Coltness, he built the ironworks at Dunaskin. These works operated very successfully until they went bankrupt in 1931. William Baird and Company took control of the assets under the newly formed Baird & Dalmellington and developed the Dunaskin site into a large-scale brickworks which continued until 1976. The site was also used by the National Coal Board as an administration centre and a coal washing plant. This, however, proved to be a short-lived venture and the site was abandoned in 1988. Fortunately, this unique industrial site was saved when in 1992 the Dunaskin Open Air Museum opened to the public. The building on the right foreground was the administrative headquarters of the National Coal Board and is now the offices of the museum. Adjacent to it is the bowling green and behind are the long rows of workers' houses. The house on the slopes of the Green Hill on the far right is called Ardoon and was the home of the ironworks' manager.

An excellent view of the extensive blast furnaces of the ironworks. The blast engines were provided in 1847 and by 1864 five were working at full capacity and plans to provide a sixth were well advanced. By the end of the 1860s there were eight. With all the furnaces in blast the disposal of the residual slag had become a major problem and when the first bogie of slag was tipped on the west side of the Dalmellington–Ayr Road at Waterside few could have imagined that the great slag hill which exists today would have been created. The last tipping of slag took place in 1921.

In the foreground of this view of the works is the line of the Glasgow & South Western Railway which is still open, carrying two train loads of coal per day from the opencast site at Minnivey. In the 1850s mines were sunk to extract the blackband ironstone for use at Waterside and the railway and its extensive networks in the area were used to transport the coal and ironstone. By the late 1850s Waterside was thriving through this combination of rail links and industry and had 237 houses. Indeed for a period after 1851 there was still insufficient accommodation at Waterside for the workers and large huts were set up to house them and sometimes their families too.

This National Coal Board 0-6-0 locomotive, No. 24, with side tanks and back bunker was built in 1953 by Andrew Barclay, Sons & Co. Ltd of Kilmarnock. Its original drivers at Waterside were Willie Clark and Willie Bryden. This engine operated as No. 8 in the West Ayr Area, but in 1964 there was an amalgamation to produce a single Ayrshire Area and some other engine had the number 8 which resulted in Waterside's No. 8 being altered to Ayrshire Area No. 24. Her crew in 1965 were Tom Bruce Jnr, driver, James Ferguson, fireman, and Hugh Hainey, guard. Today this locomotive can be seen at the Scottish Railway Preservation Society museum at Bo'ness.

National Coal Board locomotive No. 19 sitting at Waterside. This 0-4-0, with saddle tank, was built by Andrew Barclay, Sons & Co. in 1918 and arrived at Waterside in October 1919 with No. 20, bringing the total number of working engines on site to nine. Both were greatly needed as during the First World War all the engines had been exceptionally busy and were kept going with minimum repair. No. 19 was involved in several accidents. On 25 April 1929 the train had been travelling from Craigmark to Waterside and at Cutler sidings it left the line due to a points failure, resulting in the death of two men. At almost exactly the same spot in 1933, Jimmy Robertson, a guard, was killed when he was run over by wagons. On another occasion this engine went out of control and ended up crashing into wagons at the Waterside site. However, No. 19 gave long service and the last driver in 1978 was Hugh Hainey who still resides in Dalmellington. No. 19 now sits outside at Dunaskin where it can be seen by visitors entering the museum site.

The Institute, Waterside.

The Institute at Waterside was built in 1904 by the Dalmellington Iron Company as a recreation facility for the workers and their families. The building contained a reading room, games room, billiard hall with three tables, and rooms for relaxation. Children's swings and seating were provided in the grounds. This building became the Waterside Church Hall and Library in the 1950s and was also used by Dunaskin Brass Band for many years. The slag bing can be seen in the background. In the 1980s much material was removed for industrial purposes and the bing was landscaped.

Waterside Stores, *c.*1905. This was the main store run by the company to provide a large and varied range of household necessities. The building still stands today, although it is unoccupied and has been altered with the addition of an extension to the front which is shown clearly on the following page. The Waterside store was the central depot and supplies were sent from there to Craigmark and Kerse by road, while Lethanhill and Benwhat received theirs in special wagons and vans which were hauled up the rope inclines. The stores were all licensed for the sale of beer, but not for spirits. By 1876 the company had provided, staffed and maintained five schools and five stores. It was said that you could buy anything – groceries, clothes, heating, oil, furniture – in these stores and, if not in stock, it would be ordered and delivered. When workers moved house on any of the villages of the plateau, furniture was moved in the wagons pulled by a steam engine.

WATERSIDE STORES DUNASKIN.

A front view of Waterside Stores which remains largely unchanged today, although the building is no longer in use. Taken in the 1920s, this shows the extensive use made of horse and cart for transporting people and goods in the upper section of the Doon Valley. On the right of the building was the Palace Bar, a popular haunt for the hard working men of the company. Women were not welcome in such establishments. The carriage on the left is sitting on what was known locally as Parliament Corner, so called because local men gathered there and discussed the issues of the day.

Ardoon House was built overlooking the ironworks at Waterside around 1860 and was the home of the general managers of the Dalmellington Iron Company. The first to live there was John Hunter, manager from around 1848 to 1886, and he was followed by J.P. Walker (1886–1906) and Alexander Gavin (1906–1919) who had become successively secretary, general manager and managing director. The man in the photograph is Mr Stevenson, who was the gardener in the early 1900s. Today Ardoon is derelict and boarded up and the once beautiful grounds are now heavily overgrown, but a visit will reveal what a picturesque location this was.

The chapel of St Francis Xavier was opened on 14 September 1895 to serve the Catholic population in Waterside and Dalmellington, as well as 'The Hill' villages of Burnfoothill, Lethanhill, Benwhat and Corbie Craigs. The cost was £25,000, an enormous sum raised by the 500 Catholic worshippers in the district. The right hand section of the building was a school which was added in 1904. The Catholic children from 'The Hill' villages had to walk down the Waterside incline to school each day, having previously attended the schools at Burnfoothill or Benwhat. The building on the left was the Convent which was demolished in November 1994, but the remainder of the building is intact and still used as a chapel. There is an interesting statue of the Virgin Mary in the grounds which was apparently brought from France during the Second World War for safe-keeping but was never returned.

St. Francis Chapel, Dunaskin.

WATERSIDE FROM THE NORTH WEST.

A coal train at Waterside with a long rake of wagons heading for Pennyvenie. The house on the far left is Clover Park Cottage which was occupied by David Vallance, headmaster of the village school during the First World War. The next row of cottages was known as Clover Park Row. Waterside Church, next to the row, opened in 1895 and was originally a mission station operated from Dalmellington. The church is now a private residence. On the right of the church is Hillhead House and to its right is Waterside School. The row of houses to the right of the railway was known simply as the Long Row while to its right was the somewhat strangely named Monkey Row. To its right was the New Cottages. Today only Monkey Row remains, the others having been demolished in the 1950s and '60s. The slag bing to the rear show the huge amount of spoil which resulted from the production of iron ore.

Waterside looking east from the west bank of the River Doon. From right to left are the New Cottages, the Monkey Row and the Long Row. The two furnace chimneys are seen in the centre with the school left of centre. Hillhead House is next with Waterside Church on the left. The edge of the slag bing is on the extreme right.

A view of Waterside taken from high up on the slag bing. The station goods shed is at the front left with many wagons in the sidings. Waterside School is immediately above the shed with Barley Park Row behind. Barley Park Cottage is in the centre right of the picture with Greenhill Row to its right. The Waterside Institute is on the extreme right.

Patna.

The nucleus of Patna was created in 1802 when William Fullarton of Skeldon, a landowner who was born in the area and whose father had worked for the East India Company, decided that it would be a paying proposition to mine the extensive outcrops of coal in the area to the south of his estate. He named the hamlet he built to house his workers after the city in India. Fullarton later sold Skeldon Estate and moved to Ayr where twice he became provost. He died in 1835 at the age of 60. The houses of both the Long Row (centre) and the High Row (right) – both no longer standing – were occupied by local miners and their families.

Patna from The Hill Road.

M. 378.

Patna looking west from the pathway that led to 'the Hill' villages of Lethanhill and Burnfoothill, the sites of which are now part of Patna Golf Course. Taken in the 1930s, there is no extensive housing scheme to the left of the photograph as there is today. Patna remained a small village until after the Second World War when it was chosen to rehouse the residents of Lethanhill and Waterside. The row of houses on the hill to the rear is Carnshalloch Row which contained five houses. In the early 1900s limekilns were located in this area as well as coal workings which were known in this part of Ayrshire as 'ingaunees' (or 'in going eyes') with a narrow entrance where coal was extracted from shallow workings. Many such mines existed in the Doon Valley. Patna Hill, the site of the war memorial, is on the right.

By 1817 the population of Patna was big enough for the Rev. Paul of Straiton church to visit the village to conduct occasional Sunday evening services and in 1839 the parish church (in the centre of the picture) was built. On the far left of the photograph is Patna U.F. Church. This was built in 1901 by J.B. Wilson at a total cost of £2,600. Sadly this church was partially destroyed by a fire in October 1999 and it has never reopened.

Patna Bridge. M. 378.

Patna's Auld Brig was built in 1905 and the architect was Gilbert McAdam, relative of the McAdam's of Craigengillan and the engineer who gave his name to the world-famous surfacing for roads. Built in a time when the heaviest traffic would have been agricultural loads, that it has stood up well to modern traffic conditions is a tribute to its builders.

Patna Ayrshire.

The council houses on the far side of the Auld Brig were built around 1927. The other bridge at Patna, the 'New Bridge', opened in 1964 to give improved access to the extensive council housing estate built in the 1950s and 1960s.

Main Street, Patna.   M. 378.

Patna's Main Street looking east. Some of the first houses in Patna were built on the left. With the addition of an old folks' complex on the right and some modern bungalows on the left, the scene is largely unchanged today.

The Doon Hotel is situated in Main Street, Patna. This photograph was taken in the 1920s when the proprietor was William Miller and the scene is little changed today. This is the only hotel in the village and it is believed that one has been on this site from the mid-1850s.

Alexander Steel was born in 1835 and was the shoemaker in Patna for most of his working life. His small workshop was located in premises at the rear of 72 Main Street. Today they are used as an outbuilding for storage. The front bedroom of the current house was the shop where he traded as a shoemaker. He took over the business from his wife's grandfather, Thomas Dick, who died in 1867 when he was 90. Alexander Steel died in 1909 and is buried in the local cemetery.

William Alexander (1849–1921) was deaf and dumb and, in the days before political correctness, was known to many simply as the 'Patna Dummy'. Born in the parish of Dailly, he came to Patna with his father in 1851. John Hunter, manager of Dalmellington ironworks, gave him a place at the works' school and later he was apprenticed to Steele the shoemaker, before becoming a general worker at the Doon Hotel. Later he was employed for a short period at some of the Dalmellington Iron Company's collieries, and then was an odd-job man about the village until shortly before his death in 1921. Greatly respected in the district, he was buried in Patna cemetery and there was a large turnout of mourners at his funeral. He is pictured here sitting at the Walker Fountain.

The River Doon rises at Loch Enoch in the Galloway Hills and runs all the way to the Firth of Clyde at Doonfoot, Ayr. On many occasions the river floods. This particular flood at Jelliston, Patna, occurred in 1955 when the overflow pipes at Loch Doon Dam came into action when the level of the loch became dangerously high; the escaping volume of water removed pressure from the dam but large tracts of the Doon Valley were covered with water as a result.

By the end of the 1860s around 190 houses had been erected by the Dalmellington Iron Company on the plateau above Patna to accommodate the miners, and their families, working the many coal and ironstone pits in this area. The larger part was known as Lethanhill, but the row to the north, slightly apart from the others and ultimately comprising over 90 houses, was known as Burnfoothill and the whole village was more often called by this name. After a time, however, the people of the district shortened the name to the simpler title of 'the Hill.' By April 1954 all the people of 'the Hill' had been moved to the valley below and became residents of Patna and Doonbank. Many older residents of the Doon Valley fondly recall happy days living at 'the Hill' and for many years annual reunions of former residents were held.

The Low Row at Lethanhill is a typical example of the type of houses built by the Dalmellington Iron Company to house workers above Patna. After the families who lived here had been rehoused in Patna and Dalmellington, the village school remained open for several years and the children were bussed there from the villages below. There were no less than 37 ironstone pits on the plateau between Burnfoothill and Benwhat and each pit or mine was named after the farm on which it was situated. For example there were two Bowhill pits, two Polnessan pits, two Downieston pits, eleven Burnfoot pits, nine Drumgrange pits, and eight Corbie Craig pits. Of course these pits were not worked simultaneously; very often the seams were thin and the pits could sometimes be short-lived. There was also an extensive rail network on the plateau worked by steam engines brought up via several rope-worked inclines which were used to transport goods from the valley to 'the Hill'. Remains of the inclines at Burfoothill, Corbie Craigs, Drumgrange and Dunaskin can still be seen.

As well as Dalmellington and Patna, Burnfoothill, Lethanhill, Waterside, Craigmark and Benwhat all had amateur football teams. The team is Burnfoot Primrose, probably pictured in the 1920s. *Back row* (left to right): George Bowie, Adie Park, Tanny Anderson, Hugh Givens, Dummy Milligan, Buller Dalziel, Pimpy Moffot, J. Graham; *front row*: Sam Gillespie, D. Logan, S. Riddicks, Ruchie Leslie, J. McDowall, Elkie Clark, Tommy Kirk. The boy holding the shield is George Sturgeon.